BEKONSCOT

HISTORIC MODEL VILLAGE & RAILWAY

BEKONSCOT MODEL VILLAGE & RAILWAY · 80th ANNIVERSARY ·

D1067043

'A LITTLE PIECE OF HISTORY THAT IS FOREVER ENGLAND'

Right: Founder and creator of Bekonscot, Roland Callingham

WELCOME

"Would you like to come with me and visit a village so small that you will tower above the houses?" asked Enid Blyton in her 1951 book about Bekonscot, *The Enchanted Village*, which was reproduced for her centenary in 1997. Over 14 million people have visited Bekonscot; it is because of them and you that Bekonscot is here today, still raising money for charity.

Over 80 years have passed since Roland Callingham drew up plans for the world's first model village, opposite his Buckinghamshire home. The world-famous folly that has evolved as a result stands as a tribute to British eccentricity, humour, determination and craftsmanship.

It is little wonder that Bekonscot has remained so popular, for in every one of us exists a childlike curiosity for miniature things – whether it be for the tiny villages of dolls houses, patchwork of fields and gardens or the model railway, complete in every detail. Perhaps too it satisfies our desire for nostalgia and escapism; for here an idealised heritage of England exists without the unpleasant hassles of everyday modern life. Bekonscot is truly "a little piece of history that is forever England".

It was the wish of Bekonscot's founder that his village would provide simple pleasures for all; he would be very pleased that his vision lives on into the 21st century, becoming the oldest model village in the world.

The team charged with preserving Bekonscot for future generations take great pride in its upkeep. We hope that you enjoy it too.

Below: A 1951 copy of Enid Blyton's book 'The Enchanted Village' alongside the latest edition which was published in 1997. Copies of this title can be purchased a the village

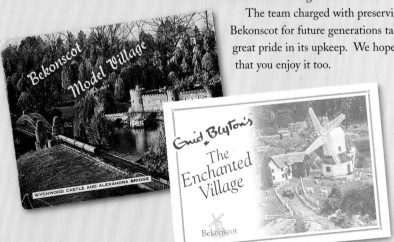

CONTENTS

THE ZOO

The rolling hills lie at your feet, with views across the fields to the villages, farms and castles beyond. Brightly-coloured houses cling to the hillsides, framed by beautiful plants, while huge figures stride across the landscape like giants. Where else could you be, but the incredible miniature world of Bekonscot, where time has stood still for more than 80 years.

As you enter this Secret Garden-like world, you will see the zoo, complete with an exotic miniature menagerie. Elephants, giraffes, penguins and flamingos are here – there is even a chimps' tea party! Like much of Bekonscot, some of these creatures are over 80 years old, carved from limewood by schoolchildren in the New Forest during the early 1930s. Chessnade, like many places at Bekonscot, is an amalgam of two real place names; in this case from two popular zoos of the era, Chessington and Whipsnade. Note the difference between how animals are kept in wildlife parks and zoos

today compared to the cramped zoos of the 1930s.

Look too at the group of houses on the right; these were rescued from Ramsgate Model Village when it closed in 2003. They have been brought back and restored here, as Bekonscot provided the inspiration for their construction in the 1960s.

Above: An ink drawing from the 1949 guidebook. Many others have been reprinted throughout this book

Top left: An inquisitive visitor and best friend explore Chessnade Zoo in 1938

Left & above: Chessnade Zoo today. Note the penguin enclosure, based on that at London Zoo

Above:
Greenhaily windmill

Main photo:
Hitting a six on the village green

GREENHAILY

The path climbs up past the bear and tiger enclosures to the highest point of the landscape. This is Greenhaily, with its coaching inn, cricket pitch, windmill and busy railway station. Listen carefully and you will hear the station master announcing the arrival and departure of trains bound for every corner of the Bekonscot district.

The Greenhaily cricket team is winning against the visitors (as usual!) from nearby Hanton. Since 1929, rain has never once stopped play in this quintessentially English sporting scene. On one side of the pitch, past the Grantley Arms inn, is the local smithy: Blacksmiths were once a vital part of village life when almost all heavy farm work was carried out by horses. The windmill on the hill above the station has long been an icon of Bekonscot, part of the logo since the very early years. Several have stood on this site, but the current one, like almost all moving models at Bekonscot is powered by electricity.

Greenhaily station is based on Beaconsfield station, which is of Great Western and Great Central Joint Line design. Here, local stopping trains can be overtaken by the expresses using the passing loops.

The lower path crosses the railway and drops down into Bekonscot Town. The upper path skims the edge of Bekonbury Castle, now a lavish stately home for a well-heeled Lord.

On the right are Greenhaily's shops; do crouch down to peek into the miniature interiors. These buildings are based on a row in the nearby town of High Wycombe; underneath lies a time capsule buried in 2000. On the left is a house under construction; having taken more than 30 years to get to this stage it is unsurprising to see that the builders are none other than 'A. Jerry'!

DID YOU KNOW:
Every newly positioned model building requires local council planning permission

Left: Greenhaily station from the road bridge with Brighton and its train passing through non-stop

Left: A horse is brought to the smithy to be shod

DID YOU KNOW:
There are more than
300 miniature animals

BEKONSCOT

This market town is the oldest part of the entire model village. Chunky, brightly-painted buildings line the High Street and side roads, where even the smallest child can look down like a giant upon the tiny people going about their daily business.

Bekonscot has all of the facilities that the most demanding resident could desire: a cinema, two railway stations, a fire station, four pubs, two market squares, a seaside pier and, of course, possibly the world's smallest Marks and Spencer.

Two real Beaconsfield pubs are depicted here: the Saracen's Head and the Earl of Bekonscot. The latter is a replica of the original Earl of Beaconsfield, which was demolished in 1981 to make way for a supermarket.

Above the town stands Clark College, the region's prestigious public school. Named after Jack Clark, an erstwhile Bekonscot engineer, it has been the site of five different buildings over the years.

Leaving the town, the road sweeps past North Bekonscot station and the almshouses, based on a prototype in nearby Amersham. An original 1929 building, the graceful minster once boasted windows by leading contemporary artist Edmund Dulac; the heavenly voices of a tiny choir still emanate from within.

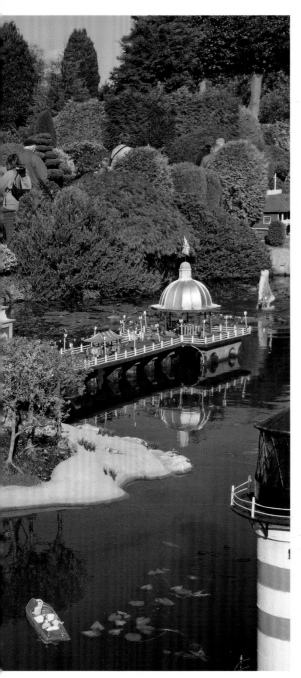

Top: Head gardener Tom Berry talks to guests in 1929

Left: The Mayor and Town Crier address a crowd in the Square

Bottom Left: Phil D. Churn the milkman makes a delivery

Look out for shop names around Bekonscot. Guess what these ones sell…

Ivan Huven
Alfred King
Evan Leigh Soles
Dan D Lyon
Mark Owney
Miss A Stitch
Argue & Twist
Lee Key
Sam & Ella

7

THE MODEL RAILWAY

The UK's finest public outdoor 'Gauge 1' (45mm gauge, 1:32 scale) model railway has weaved its way around the Bekonscot landscape for over 75 years. With almost 10 scale miles (400 real metres) of fully-signalled main line and branch line serving seven stations, the Bekonscot Model Railway (BMR) is the most intriguing part of many people's visit. There are normally between seven and ten trains running at any one time, controlled from the full-size Maryloo Signal Box. Trains run on 28V DC power.

The BMR was one of the first parts of Bekonscot to be built; it was designed and built to specification by the world-renowned Bassett-Lowke Model Railway Company. Over the years, the network grew with the additions of branches, goods yards and stock; but like British Railways it was consolidated in the 1960s as shown in photos on pages 32-33. Incredibly, the BMR has been a test-track for technology later used on many full-size railways including London Underground and Henry Greenly's 15" gauge railways.

Many of the trains have great historic value. Several of the locos have been running outdoors for more than 50 years, each covering some 2,000 real miles (3,000km) every year. The remainder are more recent constructions built in our workshops, since proprietary garden railway trains do not stand up to the rigours of seven-days-a-week running and the occasional high-speed derailment!

Like the rest of Bekonscot, the BMR was built on the whim of its creators and was never intended to accurately represent a particular prototype. Much of the rolling stock was built to freelance design, taking inspiration from many sources. Successive engineers have created a distinctively unique house style for BMR, so as an independent line, it still uses experimental liveries, locomotives and stock.

Read more about the railway, its operation and history at www.bekonscot.co.uk

LOCOMOTIVES

The locomotives and trams shown here are the ones usually available for use. Not all operate every day, and may be supplemented by stock owned by the staff. Numbers in brackets indicate construction date.

1. GK Chesterton – freelance 4-6-0 tender (1953)
2. Kew – SR 'Q class' 0-6-0 tender (1989)
3. Brighton – Bassett-Lowke 4-4-2 tank (1929)
4. Dan's Van – GWR steam railmotor (1987)
5. Settle – BR 0-6-0 pannier tank (1993)
6. Peter B – BR 0-6-0 pannier tank (1993)
7. Radstock – freelance 0-6-0 tank (1949)
8. Bruton – freelance 0-6-0 tank (1949)
9. Wells – freelance 0-6-0 tank (1949)
10. Eastbourne – SR 2BIL EMU (1999)
11. Warwick – freelance Bo-Bo diesel (1965)
12. Splashyng Tramway trams (1998)

Above: One of the many working semaphore signals

Opposite page: Far left: Trains pass at Gulley Junction

Centre left; (Top): G.K.Chesterton races through Greenhaily

(Middle): Brighton calls at Greenhaily with the stopping train

(Bottom): Eastbourne trundles along the branch line

Railway operation at
BEKONSCOT

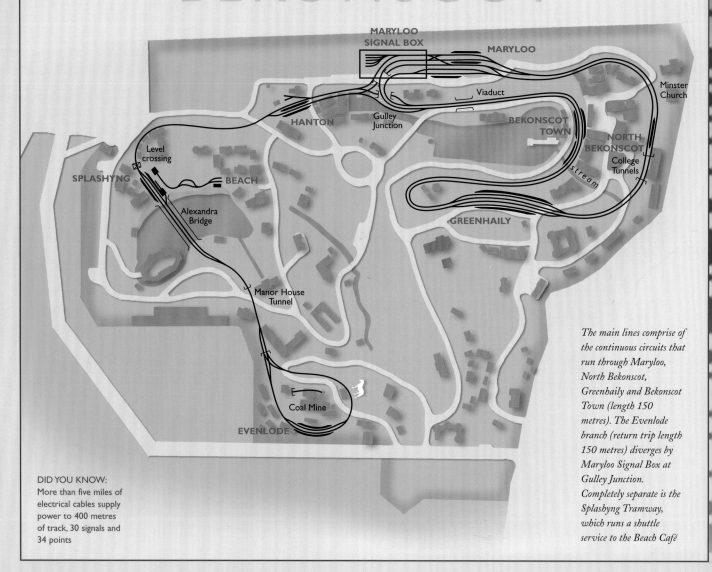

MARYLOO
SIGNAL BOX

MARYLOO

Viaduct

Minster
Church

HANTON

Gulley
Junction

BEKONSCOT
TOWN

NORTH
BEKONSCOT

College
Tunnels

Level
crossing

SPLASHYNG

BEACH

stream

Alexandra
Bridge

GREENHAILY

Manor House
Tunnel

Coal Mine

EVENLODE

The main lines comprise of
the continuous circuits that
run through Maryloo, North
Bekonscot, Greenhaily and
Bekonscot Town (length 150
metres). The Evenlode
branch (return trip length
150 metres) diverges by
Maryloo Signal Box at
Gulley Junction.
Completely separate is the
Splashyng Tramway,
which runs a shuttle
service to the Beach Café

DID YOU KNOW:
More than five miles of
electrical cables supply
power to 400 metres
of track, 30 signals and
34 points

THE SIGNAL BOX

Maryloo Signal Box is the hub of Bekonscot's railway network. From here the signalman can see the position of the trains on the system from an illuminated track diagram and can control signals and points to direct train movements by the lever frame. The signalman can also control all other moving models in the village from here.

The complex control system is one of the most advanced in the world, a fusion of historic 1930s railway engineering and 21st-century digital technology.

The railway's operation is based on real 1930s railway practice and uses a great deal of full-size equipment, such as the lever frames and relays. The working Westinghouse lever frame came from Purley signal box on British Railways and is backed up by an automated computer control system. This frame can operate the tracks around Maryloo, while outlying parts of the network are managed by the computer. The second lever frame is from Ruislip Gardens on London Underground. We are gradually restoring this cosmetically. Each train has a tiny radio beacon inside it to allow the computer to confirm and monitor its identity, location and speed. On the frame, red levers operate signals and black levers operate points.

Train crashes are rare on the BMR because the layout is divided up into many short lengths (blocks) of track, and interlocking means that only one train can be signalled into a particular block. This is similar to the principle used on 'real' railways and the entire BMR network is signalled realistically too.

Above:
The Westinghouse lever frame and illuminated diagram

Top left: A signalman prepares trains from the service pit

Bottom left: Inside the old signal box in 1950 – note the dozens of original locos and stock on the shelves

Below: A staged train crash at Greenhaily for the Evening Standard in 1937

Enid Blyton
Enid Blyton lived in Beaconsfield between 1938 and 1968. Her house, Green Hedges, was demolished, but in 1997 we built a model of it. Enid loved Bekonscot and wrote a short story, 'The Enchanted Village' all about it (see picture on page 2)

Main picture: Southpool docks
Inset: Radstock rumbles over the steel viaduct with the boat yard below

SOUTHPOOL FISHING VILLAGE

Just past the signal box, at the bottom of the cliffs, lies the sheltered harbour of Southpool, a bustling scene of activity.

Moored trawlers unload the latest catch onto the quayside, straight into the fish market or Bert Zye's van. In the 1930s, tiny ports such as this supplied the whole of the country with fish.

Beyond the quay are the rock climbers on the cliff and Southpool village, with its cottages and shops jostling for space on the steep hill. Notice some of the shop names here – I.C. Bownes is the fishmonger and Seymour Rypes is the greengrocer!

Under the railway bridge is the shipbuilding yard, where boats are being built and mended. A young Princess Elizabeth helped to launch an ocean liner here in 1936.

HANTON

Hanton is a pretty little hamlet, served by both the cliff-top tramway and the railway's branch line. The country club and maze play host to Bekonscot's more energetic and curious residents, while the picturesque church on the hill is the scene of a white wedding.

Roadworks block Evenlode Hill up to the Manor House Hotel, but there is more excitement nearby. The pretty Rose Cottage has caught fire! Thankfully the Bekonscot Fire Brigade were swiftly at the scene and are dousing down the last embers.

For the more technically minded, the steamroller is powered by pulleys and belts underneath, while the smoke in the house is provided by a proprietary gas-burning smoke machine.

Top left: A white wedding at Hanton parish church

Bottom left: The Manor House Hotel with its extensive lawns

Main photo: Firemen attack the cottage blaze

SPLASHYNG

It's market day at Splashyng and, like everywhere else, it's busy. Morris men dance in the town square and trains interrupt the traffic as they rumble over the level crossing.

Just past the station lies the goods shed where trains unload before disappearing off down the branch to Evenlode. Beyond is Alexandra Bridge; this scale model of Sydney Harbour Bridge was completed in 1945.

It's "All change!" at Splashyng for the Edwardian cliff-top tramway and planes that depart from the fashionable art deco-style airport terminal. This airfield has been wrongly-named 'Hanton' for so long, nobody has the heart to correct it!

Wychwood Castle sits surrounded by water with walls patrolled by a battalion of tiny soldiers – surely the most exciting toy fortress that any grown-up child could ever wish for. Sailing boats race around Alexandra Lake while sunbathers look on lazily from the beaches.

From the raised walkway, visitors can look straight across the landscape, to the bronze statue of Queen Victoria in the castle yard, or to the picnickers in the fields enjoying their generous hampers of ginger beer, ham sandwiches and cake.

Opposite page: Kew waits at Splashyng before heading back up the branch towards Hanton station and the main line

Left: A biplane buzzes over the luxury aircraft at Hanton airfield

Bottom left: Goods are unloaded at the shed whilst a visiting Sentinel steam loco shunts on the tramway branch

THE TUDOR HOUSE

Situated on a hill overlooking the market place of Splashyng is the Tudor House, a magnificent building which dominates this corner of the village. This house, even more than all the others, bears close scrutiny for transparent walls allow us to peer inside each of the rooms.

It is completely furnished inside, with everything from drapes and carpets to lamp stands and members of the house wearing elegant period clothes. The whole 1:12 scale house depicts a halcyon period in English history, when the local gentry lived in lavish splendour with an abundance of household servants and outdoor workers.

*Right: The canal
basin and wharf is a
hive of activity*

EVENLODE

The road between Splashyng and Evenlode affords views across to the clifftops of Alexandra Lake's Loosley Bay and Logan Bay, where another load of daytrippers arrive by clifftop tramway to play on the beach.

At the luxurious Manor House Hotel, high tea is served by fawning butlers; this is where the wealthiest of Bekonscot's residents come to relax. And the top-hatted fun of the racecourse is but a short charabanc ride along the lane!

At the heart of Evenlode is a perfect village green; children play on the swings and chase each other across the grass. A street of pretty houses tumbles across the hillside. Everyday scenes of the 1930s can be picked out: the coalman with his horse and dray and the milkman with his cart.

The path drops down steeply here to Evenlode's canal wharf. Narrowboats ply their way through the lock to the busy warehouse on the quayside, while horses drag barges along from the towpath.

It's not all hard work in the village. Over the bridge, by the Canoe Club, lies the famous fairground. The big wheel, chair-o-plane and carousel have been spinning here since the 1940s; their continued operation is a testament to the skill and craftsmanship of Bekonscot's staff. The Swiss chalet terminals of the cablecars are a nod to Bekonscot's original unofficial name – 'Little Switzerland' – when it was just a rocky alpine garden with a few buildings and people.

A hunt chases a tiny fox across the meadows of Broadwalk Lawn. Although a contentious issue today, fox hunting was an everyday part of country life in the 1930s and we have chosen to keep this original feature of Bekonscot for posterity, despite calls by some for it to be removed. Visitors should never be alarmed; our wily fox has outrun and outwitted the hounds for more than 80 years!

Opposite page:
The canal basin and
wharf is a hive of
activity

Left: The brightly-
coloured and fast-
moving models of
the fairground

Below: 1949 sketch
of Evenlode village
when all of the
buildings were half-
timbered

Far left: The swiss-
style cablecars take
daytrippers for
another ride up the
gorge
Left: A 1951 picture
shows just how
old some of the
moving fairground
models are!

17

BEKONSCOT LAKE

Bekonscot Lake is effectively Bekonscot's 'sea'. Two fast-flowing streams rush into it and a creek runs to Southpool harbour.

The scout camp, oil refinery and farm are nearby; the latter is based on the famous Ovaltine farm in Hertfordshire. Behind this is the cattle market, where farmers of the day would go to buy stock for their farms at auction. Agriculture played a much larger part in British life in the 1930s than it does now.

DID YOU KNOW:
More than 600 metres of roadways run around Bekonscot

The lake is stocked with koi carp, which must seem as big as whales to the tiny population! Brave is the fisherman who dares cast his line into these waters. Lake Drive follows the water's edge, passing W.E. Rookem's boat hire centre; here the French Brothers' steamship awaits the next load of daytrippers.

Trains rumble over Gulley Viaduct on their way to far-flung destinations across the region. The path and railway skirt the shore in a great horseshoe; the tracks detouring briefly to Bekonscot Town station. From here, the visitor can see Bekonscot's lifeboat, waterworks, lighthouse, watermill and pier. This pier, complete with theatre pavilion and enthusiastic brass band, extends across the island of St Buryan out to the sea beyond.

The lake is of particular historic interest. Its rectangular shape is not a coincidence; it was once used as a swimming pool for Roland Callingham and his friends. The spoil from its construction was used to build up the rockeries that make up the surrounding hills.

Left: A 1960s painted photo postcard of Bekonscot Pier. At the time it was open to the public, but later altered

Below: Bekonscot Yacht Haven and quayside beyond

EVENLODE NEW TOWN & COLLIERY

Above: Safety first? Not at Evenlode's petroleum filling station!

Passing alongside the immaculate Broadwalk Lawn, a church is seen to the left. This is a model of St Theresa's, which is located at the entrance of Bekonscot's car park. The model was completed in 1937, before the original!

The road continues past the zoo and uphill to the garage where the most modern of motor cars are under repair; this path now twists down into a rocky valley with the mining town ahead.

Bekonscot Coal Board's Evenlode New Town is a recent addition, built in 2003. This settlement, like many Victorian mining towns in Britain, was built by the mining companies to house the many workers who toiled away underground in treacherous conditions.

Far right: Another busy day at the coal mine

Collieries like this were once a common sight; during the early 20th century over one million people worked in more than 500 mines to supply Britain's industries, railways and homes with coal. Now less than a dozen pits are left.

HOW THE COLLIERY WORKS

Many visitors are amazed to see that the colliery produces tiny lumps of real coal, which appear to have been brought from underground, then transported on conveyors to the waiting trains. In reality, sadly, Beaconsfield has very little coal to be mined! The coal produced by the BCB is delivered by a local coal merchant and is put in a silo inside the sorting building. This is transported to the coal wagons by two conveyors. Dropping down the chute, the coal falls through the railway wagon's floor onto another conveyor; this takes the coal back into the sorting building for another circuit.

Above: Fresh fruit for sale in Evenlode New Town

EPWOOD

Epwood is our last stop on the tour that is the rural timewarp that is the Bekonscot district. It is home to the once-grand Epwood Castle on Epwood Downs, a timber yard and a polo pitch (the high point of every Bekonscot socialite's calendar!).

In the copse that abuts the fortress walls is a clearing where bodgers are at work ('bodger' was the local name given to men who made wooden furniture for a living; often inhabiting the woodlands in which they worked). In the 1930s, Buckinghamshire was an important centre for furniture-making; the nearby town of High Wycombe was famous for its high-quality wooden chairs.

At the centre of the boating pond is a tiny island, on which an obelisk stands, dedicated to Roland Callingham, Bekonscot's founder. Without his vision and imagination, Bekonscot would not exist – this magical little world would be just another suburban housing estate.

Above: Bodgers hard at work

Left: A polo match

DID YOU KNOW:
Bekonscot has a miniature population of 3,000

THE WORKSHOPS

Around the edge of the village are several workshops where a dozen modelmakers and engineers design, build and maintain the models. It is because of their passion and skill that the trains, moving models, gardens, miniature buildings and people have been preserved, and that new exhibits appear each year. Although these workshops are too hazardous for public access, here you can catch a glimpse into what goes on behind closed doors.

There are five specialist workshops: Engineering, Modelmaking, Model People, Carpentry and Gardens. Each team is responsible for maintenance and innovation in that area. They constantly experiment with new materials so that quality, durability and detail improve each year.

Much of what you see is over 80 years old: we do our utmost to keep this wonderful heritage perfect for future generations to enjoy. Although some stone and cast concrete buildings are originals from 1929, others are replaced every ten years. As the village ages and we run out of room for new models, maintenance is becoming increasingly important.

Left: Finishing
touches are
added to the
Ascot
Racecourse
buildings

WHAT HAPPENS IN WINTER?

Bekonscot is closed during the winter months for refurbishment, which is when larger construction and maintenance projects are undertaken – the site becomes too dangerous for public access. All of the smaller models are taken indoors and refurbished but the hardy railway and main buildings stay outside.

Even a light dusting of snow causes huge drifts for the Bekonscot residents – this problem of scale also causes issues for one particular visitor every Christmas!

DID YOU KNOW: Most new buildings are made with a wood frame and a layer of carved dense foamboard

Right: St Teresa's church surrounded by a mass of flowering bedding plants

Below: Some examples of the scaled-down topiary

THE GARDENS

Over the years the gardens have developed into an outstanding feature of the model village. There are now well over 3,000 shrubs and trees in scale with the models; many of these appear to be bonsai-style. They are, however, not strictly 'bonsai', but skilfully trimmed and gradually re-shaped standard garden plants. Many of these were a feature of the original Bekonscot alpine gardens. Some of the most-used varieties include Japanese maples, Japanese elms, miniature willows, cypress, ficus and lilacs.

Bekonscot is a riot of colour during the summer, the models framed by thousands of bedding and herbaceous plants. An immaculate stretch of lawn runs the length of the village, which was originally part of the meadow from which Bekonscot was created. It is known as 'Broadwalk Lawn', because when Roland Callingham first built Bekonscot, he would walk along it twice daily on his way to and from the railway station.

The lakes of Bekonscot are much-admired by visitors. These ponds and waterways are stocked with dozens of koi carp, mostly donated to us by kind visitors. Suspended over the lakes are several thin wires – these deter herons from stealing the fish!

BEKONSCOT LIGHT RAILWAY

The Bekonscot Light Railway (BLR) is our passenger-carrying narrow gauge railway. Built to a gauge of $7^1/_4$ inches, it is often mistaken for a miniature railway but is actually just a very small track width with large locomotives and rolling stock. The inspiration for the BLR came from the concept of Sir Arthur Heywood's estate railways of the late nineteenth century, which aimed to convey passengers and goods on the smallest gauge possible.

Opened in 2001, the BLR weaves its way behind the model village, criss-crossing and looping around itself past ponds and hidden gardens. The trip is short – but almost impossible to see where you're going next!

The BLR has been laid partly on the route of Bekonscot's original internal narrow gauge railway, used by the contractors during construction in 1928. We discovered the remnants of this line in 2001 and have preserved its wagons (see page 26).

There are currently four locomotives that regularly haul trains on the BLR; all are battery-powered. Track has been bought in but laid to our own route design; this has required extremely tight curves of a 20ft radius. Future developments include more rolling stock, full signalling and more unusual scenery along the route.

Below: In 2008 we introduced radio-controlled boats by the lineside

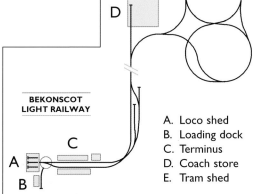

BEKONSCOT LIGHT RAILWAY

A. Loco shed
B. Loading dock
C. Terminus
D. Coach store
E. Tram shed

No.1 "Sprocket"
0-4-0 Battery Electric
Built 2001: Maxitrak Ltd
Hudson Hunslet diesel outline

No.3 "The Tram"
Bo-Bo Battery Electric
Built 2001: Bekonscot Eng. Dept.
Freelance outline tram

No. 5 "Bouncer"
Bo-Bo Battery Electric
Built 2007: Bekonscot Eng. Dept.
Freelance shunting loco

In 2009 we introduced No.6, a Bo-Bo Diesel Hydraulic, built by the Bekonscot Engineering Department. This advanced shunting loco has been developed to cope with our tight curves, heavy loads and gradients. Keep an eye out for her and other new stock!

CONSTRUCTION

In 1927, Roland Callingham, a London accountant, instructed contractors to dig a swimming pool at his home in Beaconsfield, Buckinghamshire. The pool and his tennis courts were used for garden parties, attended by the high society of London.

In 1928, Roland's indoor model railway finally outgrew his home, so he commissioned model railway firm Basset-Lowke to build the largest outdoor Gauge 1 garden railway in England. In his spare time Roland, with his head gardener Tom Berry, built some model houses to complement it; the pool then gained two islands and a pier. When the summer evenings grew too dark to play tennis, party guests would wander over to play with the model trains and swim in the pool. Guests still swam in this 'sea' as late as 1935!

Encouraged by friends and house staff, Roland planned a rural landscape surrounding the pool, railway and rockeries with boundless passion. His team, including local schoolboys, turned their hands to modelmaking and the construction of Bekonscot town. Half-timbered and stone houses, shops and castles sprang out of the rockeries with a network of tiny roads to connect them.

Local buildings and personal favourites of the staff provided much of the village's inspiration, for all were constructed from memory and photos.

Bekonscot's founder was never concerned with precision or 'rivet-counting'. Bekonscot was, and always will be, eccentric, fun and full of character; it was never meant to be taken seriously.

BACK FROM THE GRAVE!

In 2001, while digging to replace a retaining wall, staff unearthed three full-sized 2ft gauge wagons. Research indicates that they were used on a contractor's railway to build Bekonscot, and later transported goods around the site. Thought to be of Hudson design, all have been restored and one is on display in the picnic area. Later excavations showed that Clark College is built on a plinth, supported by the wagons' old tipper-truck bodies. What else lurks under Bekonscot?

BY ROYAL APPOINTMENT

Bekonscot has welcomed members of the British and overseas royal families many times over the years. The first visit was on 20 April 1934, the eve of Princess Elizabeth's eighth birthday. She returned several times in later years with Princess Margaret, Queen Mary and the King, a series of personal letters between Roland Callingham and the royal household indicate that Bekonscot was always a favourite destination. After her coronation, the Queen's children came too and were equally enthralled by the beauty of this, the smallest of Kingdoms.

FAME!

Following suggestions from friends and family, Roland opened Bekonscot to the public in 1929. The village was seen in newspapers, newsreels and magazines across the world, and thousands flocked to see the 'real-life Lilliput'.

No admission charge was made, but the public were invited to put money in collection-boxes for charity if they wished. In 1932, however, the Bekonscot Model Railway & General Charitable Association was set up to administer the village and distribute surplus money to charity.

With Bekonscot's growing popularity, the public opening hours were extended from occasional days to weekend openings too. For a while, there were open evenings when every building and path was lit up with tiny twinkling electric lights. As visitor numbers increased, paths were widened and more buildings such as Epwood Castle and Evenlode were added.

Members of Roland Callingham's household staff, including his cook, gardeners, chauffeur and maid, all came to help run the model village.

Above: 1935 advertisement for the village

Left: Princess Elizabeth in 1934 Inset: Princess Alexandra, Duke of Kent, Prince Michael and friends in 1945

Left: A busy day in 1936

DID YOU KNOW: Almost 15 million people have visited since 1929

BEKONSCOT GROWS UP

Following the continued success of the original model village area, it was decided to significantly increase its size. Previously, the village comprised Bekonscot town, Greenhaily windmill, Evenlode and Southpool docks. In 1945, the village of Splashyng was founded. Alexandra Lake was dug out and a likeness of Sydney Harbour Bridge was built to span the water and carry the branch railway out to Evenlode.

At this time, a variety of scales were used for model-making. Trains were 1:32 scale, houses and people were 1:12 whilst large buildings and boats were as big as the space would allow. It was decided to pursue a uniform scale thereafter of 1:12, now the world-standard for dolls houses, but the model railway was too well-established to be changed. To this day, very few people notice that the trains are less than half the correct size for their surroundings!

More complex, modern and detailed buildings were constructed, while the villages grew from tiny hamlets to include industries, an airfield and more railway lines. At one stage, there was almost double today's track length of 400 metres.

Above: A crowd gathers for the opening of Hanton airfield in 1936. Roland Callingham is on the far right

Right: An early photo of Bekonscot's minster church

Below right: One of the first trains over Alexandra bridge in 1945

Opposite page: Maryloo in 1932. Note the three-rail track and original Bassett-Lowke stock. Two of the coaches are still in use today!

BEKONSCOT AT WAR

Most of Bekonscot's staff left in 1939 to fight in the Second World War. Tragically, not all returned. The model village, embodying everything quintessentially English, was used for a series of propaganda pictures during the war. Model warships were depicted shooting down Nazi aircraft, while head gardener Tom Berry is shown here in Epwood Castle, defending king and country.

Above: A fox is hunted in 1947

Right: The Queen Mary is carried to her annual launch in 1948

Opposite page;
Top: Wilson Carlile, founder of the Church Army, visiting in 1934

Middle: One of many TV appearances was made when Muffin the Mule visited in 1955

Bottom: By 1966, concrete structures and diesel trains had taken over. Compare with the 2003 view on page 12

PRESERVED FOR ALL TIME

The Second World War left Bekonscot, like the outside world, in a bad way. Maintenance had all but stopped, materials were hard to acquire and most staff were away fighting. In 1948, an ambitious rebuilding programme rejuvenated or replaced many of the derelict buildings, maintaining the rural atmosphere.

Now surrounded by residential suburbia, in 1952 Bekonscot won a three-year court battle with the town planners, permitting it to remain open to the public. The village and its tiny population grew, as did its popularity and charity fundraising, under the auspices of Roland and his team, most of whom now worked full-time at Bekonscot. It was at this time that other model villages began to appear (see page 34).

Roland Callingham, gentleman, philanthropist, designer and grandfather of the world's model villages, died in 1961. For another 15 years, Tom Berry and his staff kept Roland's dream alive, but rather than standing still, time moved on at Bekonscot. More modern buildings, cars and trains appeared, reflecting the contemporary world outside.

A turning point was reached in 1976 when the Church Army was approached to assist with the running of Bekonscot. Since 1934 the charity had been one of the

major beneficiaries of Bekonscot's fundraising, and its founder, Wilson Carlile, shared Roland Callingham's philanthropic ideals.

Just in time for the village's Golden Jubilee in 1979, a rolling programme of improvements was introduced which saw new scenes added, overgrown hamlets rediscovered and older buildings restored. Notable events included the construction of the coal mine, installation of the Westinghouse lever frame at Maryloo, and the Mk I coach being delivered for use as a souvenir shop.

In 1992, riding on a wave of regained popularity and interest in heritage, the decision was taken to return Bekonscot to its former glory: the heydays of the 1930s. Deteriorating models were rebuilt or replaced sympathetically, while others were backdated to their original 1930s styling. The model railway was completely reconstructed, incorporating the old signalling system into a complex computer-controlled network, all of which was housed in a brand new replica signal box. A deeper political agenda has been suggested to be behind the changes by some commentators. But perhaps to analyse it too deeply is to destroy Bekonscot's real agenda; Bekonscot is a place of fun, enjoyment and whimsical eccentricity – and it always will be.

Seen through 21st-century eyes, it is perhaps best to see the village in the context of its history, as it stubbornly refuses to modernise. Bekonscot has done what we would all like to do: it has never aged and it has never really grown up. Bekonscot is truly a little piece of history that is forever England; we hope that Roland would be proud.

Above: A miniature newspaper (shown half size here) to commemorate Bekonscot's 50th birthday

Left: The obelisk dedicated to Bekonscot's founder, Roland Callingham

1929

1947

The Village and Coll

EVOLUTION OF BEKONSC

MARYLOO STATION BEKONSCOT. 804

1929

1951

1970

2008

WN & MARYLOO STATION

1981

2008

THE LEGACY OF BEKONSCOT

Bekonscot is the model village that has inspired all others since – it is the oldest surviving model village in the world. The popularity of Bekonscot led to the construction of many model villages across Britain – one early example was Bourton-on-the-Water, which opened in 1937 and still operates to this day. Like Bekonscot it had large-scale buildings lining the pathways, giving visitors the feeling that they were giants wandering down the streets; modern model villages or miniature parks usually take the form of individual scenes set in pre-planned gardens.

The Dobbins brothers took a notable interest in Bekonscot and visited many times to work with Callingham's team. The superb villages at Babbacombe, Southport and Great Yarmouth were formed as a result. Stan Deboo, a Bekonscot modelmaker, was instrumental in many villages across Kent and beyond. Other resorts saw the commercial opportunities and at one time several dozen existed. Babbacombe, Godshill, Wimborne, Corfe Castle, Bridlington and Great Yarmouth are a few that have survived the test of time. We urge you to visit these other miniature masterpieces. Most, like Ramsgate and Tucktonia, fell on hard times and closed. Incidentally, in early 2004, we repatriated and restored some of the Ramsgate houses; these are now displayed by Chessnade Zoo in a way typical of the 1960s model villages: set away from the paths, arranged in an open display.

Highly successful miniature parks have opened up across the world, including Madurodam in the Netherlands and Mini Europe in Brussels. More recently, interest in model villages has been re-ignited and ventures such as the Forest Model Village in Gloucestershire have appeared. Despite differences in scale, size, culture and prosperity, it is clear that the legacy of Bekonscot and Roland Callingham lives on, entertaining adults and children the world over.

*Clockwise:
Brochure for
Merrivale at Great
Yarmouth; the vast
but now-demolished
Tucktonia at
Christchurch near
Bournemouth; the
high street of the
now-closed Ramsgate;
and the relocated and
restored Ramsgate
cottages back at
Bekonscot*

DID YOU KNOW:
At today's rates, Bekonscot has raised more than four million pounds for charity

IAMP

Bekonscot is a member of IAMP, the International Association of Miniature Parks. The association has been formed to promote co-operation between model villages worldwide and to facilitate greater awareness of the attractions themselves. Through IAMP, Bekonscot has had models displayed at venues across Europe.

There are currently almost 20 member parks in Europe, Asia and Australasia, who meet up every year to discuss industry issues and share ideas. In 2004, IAMP came to Bekonscot to celebrate the 75th anniversary of the world's oldest and longest-running model village: the one that inspired them all.

Further information is available at www.miniatureparks.org

VISIT US ON THE INTERWEB!

Even Bekonscot had to join the 21st century some time, so we've been building an interweb netsite thing from bits of wood, nails and leftovers from the signalbox. We think it's jolly good. Click your mouse pointer-thing on your PC machine to:

www.bekonscot.co.uk

...and you'll find some rather super things for both small people and not-so-small people. Our workshop people say that you can:

- Build your own model village on the Virtual Village
- See exclusive videos and archive photographs
- Take behind-the-scenes virtual tours of the workshops
- Join our newsletter for regular updates, offers and things (do sign up and tell your friends – occasionally we send out some very interesting stories and news from the village).

The Virtual Village

CREDITS AND ACKNOWLEDGEMENTS

This book is a tribute to the team who have made, and continue to make, Bekonscot one of the most remarkable places in Britain: may Bekonscot inspire many generations in the future. Thanks must go to all the people who have supported and assisted production of this book.

© 2009 Bekonscot Model Village and Jarrold Publishing.
Author: Tim Dunn.

Main photography by Jarrold Publishing.
Additional photography by Tim Dunn, Tim Baker and Merve Hill
Archive photography © Bekonscot Model Village.
Design, model railway plan and village plan by Richard Crossley.

Designed and produced by Jarrold Publishing, part of the Heritage House Group, Norfolk
ISBN 978-0-85101-435-7

Printed in Great Britain. B-81658-2/09

JARROLD
publishing

A map of
BEKONSCOT
Historic Model Village & Railway

First Aid

Toilets

Refreshments Kiosk

Tudor House

Picnic Area

Shelter

Raised Walkway

SPLASHYNG

Log Cabin

Wychwood Castle

Racecourse

Play Area

Picnic Area

Splashyng Station

Aerodrome

Farmyard

HANTON

Tramway

Lake

Hotel

Shelter

Evenlode New Town

Evenlode Station

Shelter

Workshop

EVENLODE

Coal Mine

Archaeology site

Shelter

Enid Blyton's House

Hanton Station

SOUTHPOOL

Fairground

canal

Waterfalls & Cable Car

Polo

Epwood Castle

Bodgers

Radio-controlled Boats

Golf Club

Hunt

Relay Room

Signal Box

Maryloo Station

School

Windmill

Greenhaily Station

GREENHAILY

Cricket pitch

Zoo

Ramsgate Houses

IN

OUT (or around again!)

Minster Church

Bekonscot Town Station

Lake

Pier

Water Mill

BEKONSCOT

stream

North Bekons Station

Bekonbury Castle

TO SHOP & Light Railway Station

Picnic storage shed

Shelter

BEKONSCOT LIGHT RAILWAY

Bekonscot Model Village, Warwick Road, Beaconsfield, Buckinghamshire HP9 2P
Telephone: 01494 672919 **Fax:** 01494 675284
Website: www.bekonscot.co.uk **Email:** info@bekonscot.co.uk

ISBN 978-0-85101-435-7

9 780851 014357

'A LITTLE PIECE OF HISTORY THAT IS FOREVER ENGLAND'